P9-DED-194

Mercedes and the Chocolate Pilot

A TRUE STORY OF THE BERLIN AIRLIFT AND THE CANDY THAT DROPPED FROM THE SKY

By Margot Theis Raven

Illustrated by Gijsbert van Frankenhuyzen

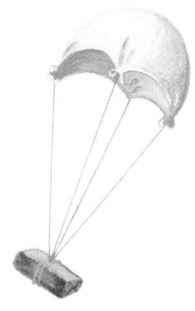

To the children of Berlin, the children of the World, and the children of Heaven,
especially Nick Ressler, who knew the power in a stick of gum.

—MTR

To those who preserve our freedom.

—GSH

Sleeping Bear Press™

2395 South Huron Parkway, Suite 200
Ann Arbor, MI 48104
www.sleepingbearpress.com

Printed and bound in the United States.

25 24 23 22 21 20 (case)

Library of Congress Cataloging-in-Publication Data
Raven, Margot Theis.
Mercedes and the Chocolate Pilot / by Margot Theis Raven
p. cm.
Summary: The true story of a young German girl, Mercedes Simon, and of the American pilot Gail Halvorsen, who
shares hope and joy with the children of West Berlin by dropping candy-filled parachutes during the Airlift.

ISBN: 978-1-58536-069-7 case

1. Berlin (Germany)—History—Blockade, 1948-1949—Juvenile literature. 2. Halvorsen, Gail S.—Juvenile literature. 3. United States. Air Force.
Military Airlift Command—Biography—Juvenile literature. 4. Air pilots. Military—United States—Biography—Juvenile literature. 5. Simon,
Mercedes—Juvenile literature. 6. Girls— Germany—Berlin—Biography—Juvenile literature. [1. Berlin (Germany)—History—Blockade, 1948-
1949—Juvenile literature. 2. Halvorsen, Gail S. 3. Simon, Mercedes. 4. United States. Air Force. Military Airlift Command—Biography. 5. Air
Pilots, Military 6. World War, 1939-1945—Germany. 7. Germany—History—1945-1955.] 1. Title.
DD881.R382002   943'.1550874—dc21   2002001887

Additional letters and first-hand accounts of the Chocolate Pilot can be found in his book,
***The Berlin Candy Bomber*. Order information is available at: wigglywings@juno.com**

Further information about Colonel Halvorsen and the Berlin Airlift can be found on the
Berlin Airlift Veterans Association web page at: www.konnections.com/airlift/candy.htm

AUTHOR'S NOTE

This book exists through the generous support and blessings of Col. Gail S. Halvorsen USAF (Ret.) and Mercedes Wild, Berlin, Germany. Thank you both from the depths of my heart for the honor and privilege of telling your story.

Thank you also to the following individuals and friends who went out of their way to help gather and give important information: Peter Wild (Berlin, Germany); Col. Kenneth Herman USAF (Ret.), past-president of the Berlin Airlift Veterans Association; Gudrun Fruehling, president and managing editor, Armed Forces Journal International; Christa Borgman, German language specialist; Ken Sansom; and Karin, Klaus, Marcel, and Frau Lilo Besier, caring neighbors.

Thank you also to my agent, Andrea Brown, for supporting this project from the very beginning, and a heartfelt thank you to my editor, Heather Hughes, associate editor Barb McNally, and publicist Mary Ann Riehle, for believing in the goodness of this story and getting its message out so quickly.

Lastly, a most loving thank you to my brother-in-law, Bob Weed, for your magical touch; my son, Scott, for our Adobe sessions; my husband, Greg, for your loving help in Washington; and most especially to my daughter, Ashley, who shared the book's creation with me, from our trip to Utah to making endless weekends of photocopying so much fun!

—MARGOT THEIS RAVEN

I offer my undying gratitude to my dear friend, Mercedes, and to the exceptional professionals who captured the magic of her struggle to be free: author, Margot Raven; illustrator, Gijsbert van Frankenhuyzen; and team Sleeping Bear Press.

—COLONEL GAIL HALVORSEN

ILLUSTRATOR'S NOTE

As always, I would like to thank the models who helped me with my book. Ustina Treber Shives, a beautiful girl inside and out. You make a wonderful Mercedes. Ben Winkel, actor/body double. From Cornell Elementary, Ron McCurdy's fourth grade class and from Gunnisonville Elementary, John Shives's fifth grade class. Most of all, my gratitude and respect to Colonel Gail Halvorsen and his gracious wife, Lorraine, for sharing their home and hospitality with me. The stories you shared helped make the book what it is. A story of hope, love, and forgiveness.

—GIJSBERT VAN FRANKENHUYZEN

There is no discussion. We stay in Berlin. Period!

President Harry S. Truman
June 28, 1948

THE BERLIN AIRLIFT

The Berlin Airlift of 1948-1949 is still one of the greatest humanitarian missions the world has ever known. Like a great sky bridge, airplanes flew 24 hours a day, three minutes apart, to feed 2.2 million people for 15 desperate months.

It began three years after WWII had ended, when defeated Germany and its capital, Berlin, were carved into four pieces like a pie by the Allied countries who had conquered Adolf Hitler's army. Josef Stalin's Soviet Union (Russia) controlled the eastern sector of Berlin as well as East Germany. Great Britain, the United States, and France controlled the three western sectors of Berlin as well as West Germany.

At first, all four Allies ruled Germany in friendship, but on the fateful day of June 24, 1948, Josef Stalin tried to take both East and West Berlin for himself so he could eventually put all of Germany, then all of Europe, under his communist government. Since Berlin sat 110 miles deep within Russia's territory, Stalin simply had to blockade the roads, railroads, and canal routes coming in and out of the city to cut off West Berliners from food, clothing, heat, and electricity.

What could the Allies do? If they freed West Berlin with guns and tanks there would be another world war! Only three air corridors, each 20 miles wide, were still open for the U.S., Great Britain, and France to utilize. And so the idea for the incredible sky bridge began.

From June 26th, 1948 to September 30th, 1949, the British and American forces flew more than 277, 000 missions, day and night, delivering more than 2.3 million tons of supplies. This is the same distance as going back and forth between the earth and the moon 130 times!

To keep people alive, Berlin needed 4,500 tons of food, coal, and essentials daily! Imagine packing, carrying, and unloading 646 tons of flour and wheat per day; 180 tons of dehydrated potatoes; 19 tons of powdered milk; 5 tons of fresh milk for babies and small children; 109 tons of meat and fat; 125 tons of cereal; and combined, over 5,000 tons of coal and kerosene during the summer and winter. And many other essential items were part of the cargo!

Nothing was easy about this rescue mission and there were many problems: the weather was terrible; the runways short; the skies crowded; the pilots had little sleep; Russian planes harassed the exhausted fliers in the air corridors; coal and flour dust caused mechanical problems.

The greatest cost of the operation was the loss of lives: 31 Americans died, 39 British, and 9 Germans. But they are not forgotten. In Berlin today, the memory of the beautiful "bridge" is cherished by the people who love their freedom, and remember the brave pilots and the countries who did not forsake them in their time of need.

This is the true story of a seven-year-old girl named Mercedes Simon who lived in the city of West Berlin during the airlift and of the American pilot who came to be known as the Chocolate Pilot.

BERLIN 1948

One late August day, Mercedes slipped her hand under the white chickens she kept in the small courtyard garden behind her apartment building.

Please let there be eggs, she wished as the silver-winged planes flew above like guardian angels. But like yesterday and the day before, the chickens' nests were empty, except for one small egg.

Mercedes fed each chicken a worm and tried not to cry. She loved her four feathered pets, but Mama would not be happy. Eggs were more precious than gold in West Berlin during the Russian blockade.

"Tomorrow I want an egg from each of you," she scolded the chickens sternly, "or Mama will say we cannot afford to keep you and must have you for dinner instead!"

Walking up the bomb-splintered steps to her apartment, Mercedes was sure her white chickens were just too scared of the thundering planes of the airlift to lay their eggs.

Night and day they roared overhead like huge silver birds into nearby Tempelhof Air Field to unload their supplies. But Mercedes would never complain about the great soaring grocery stores that everyone called *Raisinbombers*, because they carried yummy raisins to eat! They carried flour and clothing and coal too. And something else!

One day Mama read her a newspaper story about the candy that came from the planes. The story told about the wonderful American Chocolate Pilot, Lt. Gail Halvorsen. Every day, he rained down sweets on the children who cheered the planes landing on Tempelhof's runway.

As Mama read, Mercedes learned how the tall, friendly pilot had talked with these children one day at the fence near the runway's end.

"The children didn't ask him for candy," Mama read, "only sweet freedom. Still, before he had to go, he searched his pocket for gum. But he found only two sticks — and there were 30 children!"

"What did he do, Mama?" Mercedes asked.

"He split the sticks for four lucky children," Mama read, "and the others tore slivers of the foil to smell as their sweet treats. Then, even though he knew he could get in terrible trouble, the pilot promised the children he would drop gum and candy to them from his plane the next day! He stretched out his arms and told them to look for the wiggle of his plane's wings."

"That night the pilot made small candy-filled parachutes from handkerchiefs," Mama read on, "and dropped them in secret to the children at the airfield the next day. He made three candy drops after that, before his troubles began!"

"Children's letters addressed to *The Chocolate Pilot* and *Uncle Wiggly Wings* began to arrive at the airfield. Then a candy bar almost hit a reporter on his head, and the colonel in charge at Tempelhof read about the pilot's secret in the newspaper! He was caught!"

"Did the colonel yell at him?" Mercedes cringed, but Mama laughed and said, "Only a little, then he shook his hand and told him to 'keep dropping and keep him informed!'"

"But won't he run out of candy?" Mercedes asked anxiously, but Mama laughed again.

"People from all over America now send the pilot handkerchiefs for parachutes, and so much candy that it fills two large railroad boxcars!"

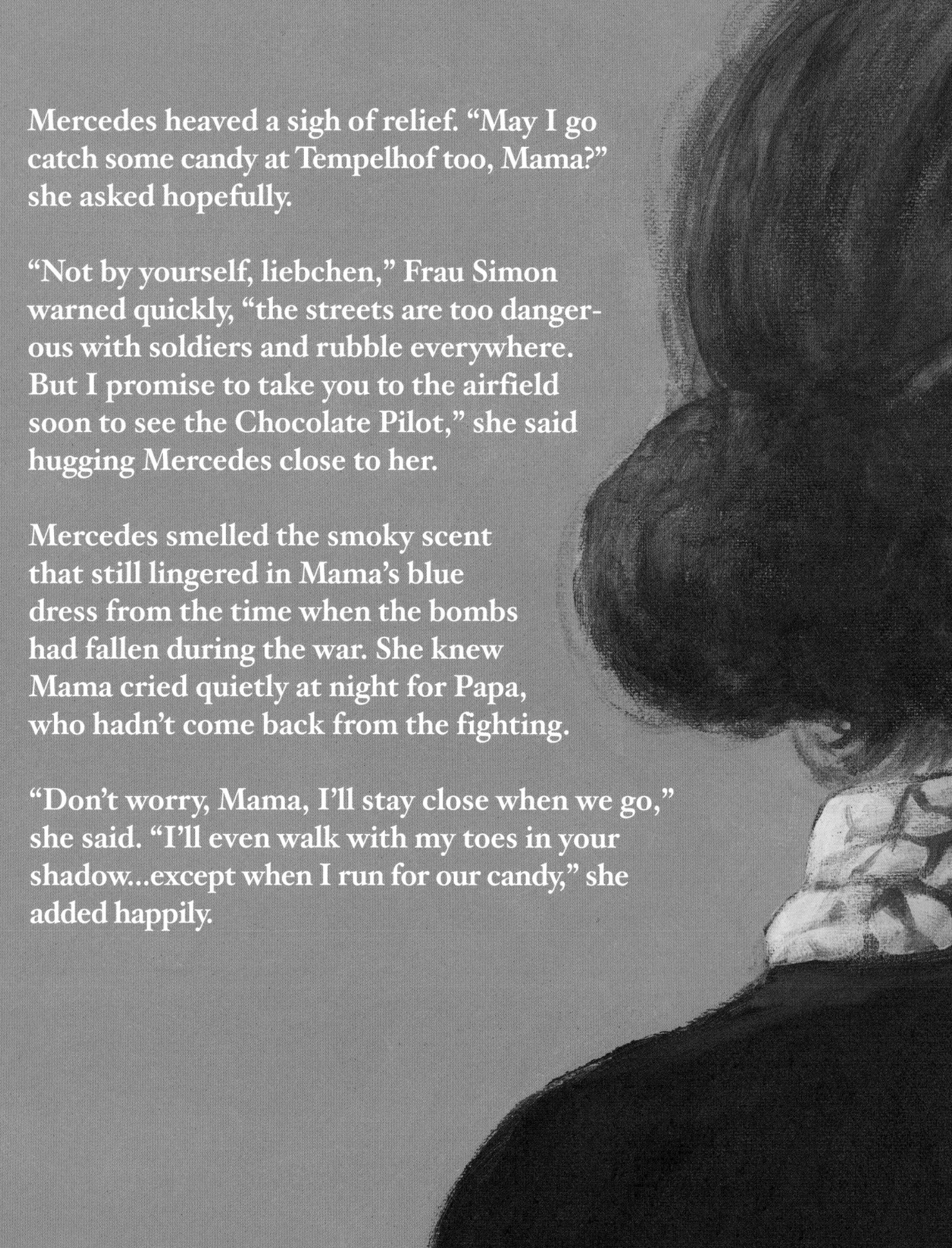

Mercedes heaved a sigh of relief. "May I go catch some candy at Tempelhof too, Mama?" she asked hopefully.

"Not by yourself, liebchen," Frau Simon warned quickly, "the streets are too danger-ous with soldiers and rubble everywhere. But I promise to take you to the airfield soon to see the Chocolate Pilot," she said hugging Mercedes close to her.

Mercedes smelled the smoky scent that still lingered in Mama's blue dress from the time when the bombs had fallen during the war. She knew Mama cried quietly at night for Papa, who hadn't come back from the fighting.

"Don't worry, Mama, I'll stay close when we go," she said. "I'll even walk with my toes in your shadow...except when I run for our candy," she added happily.